Office Genius

Summersdale Publishers Ltd
46 West Street
Chichester
West Sussex
PO19 1RP
UK

www.summersdale.com

Printed and bound in the Czech Republic

ISBN: 978-1-84953-483-3

Substantial discounts on bulk quantities of Summersdale books are available to corporations, professional associations and other organisations. For details contact Nicky Douglas by telephone: +44 (0) 1243 756902, fax: +44 (0) 1243 786300 or email: nicky@summersdale.com.

Office Genius

An Innovative Approach To Office Life

James Andrews

summersdale

Newton's Cradle of Blame

A Beautiful Gift for the Office for Just £39

Newton's Cradle of Blame is a beautifully crafted desktop accessory specially designed for people in management positions. Based on the original Newton's Cradle, Newton's Cradle of Blame authentically replicates the transfer of blame through an organisation using seven hand-finished die-cast figurines, each one performing an instantly recognisable gesture.

What's more, you can add a personal touch to your Cradle of Blame by sellotaping your staff's faces directly onto the figurines.

This is Sally Barnes, everybody, she'll be taking over from Simon. I think you'll find us all pleasant enough people to work with, Sally - Peter, have you got the sellotape?

Let yourself go and let yourself down with

Office Dance Party II

As a manager, your staff expect you to dance ridiculously at the office Christmas party - you expect it of yourself. And now you need never disappoint, thanks to Office Dance Party II.

Office Dance Party II contains all the outdated, badly performed and sexually inappropriate dance moves you need to dance hilariously in front of your staff this Christmas. From entry-level John Travolta impersonations right through to advanced-level crotch grabbing and jaw-dropping techno solos, we'll teach you all the moves you need to look ridiculous and make others feel awkward on your behalf this Christmas.

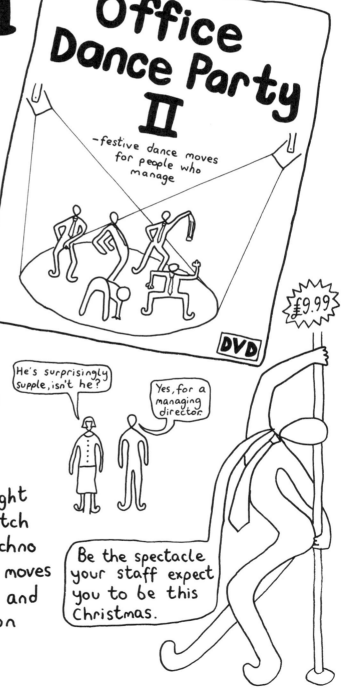

Office Dance Party II
- festive dance moves for people who manage

DVD

£9.99

He's surprisingly supple, isn't he?

Yes, for a managing director

Be the spectacle your staff expect you to be this Christmas.

Improve Staff Access to the Photocopier with a

Photocopier Stepladder

Taking a photocopy of yourself sitting on the work's copier and passing it round the office is a perfectly normal and accepted part of office employment. But are you risking serious injury having to mount the copier from swivel chairs and upturned wastepaper bins? If so, perhaps it's time you asked for a Photocopier Stepladder.

The Photocopier Stepladder is the perfect way to access the work's photocopier without risking serious injury. Non-slip feet and a grab rail afford excellent stability through difficult transitions on and off the copier, whilst six treaded steps provide easy access to hard-to-reach desk-mounted copiers. Ask your line manager for a Photocopier Stepladder today!

Only £48

These colour copies could land me in trouble...

...but at least I'm safe.

Have you got much to do?

Cheeky Sod!

Office Review:

"We're experiencing far fewer photocopier-related accidents – admittedly, though, we are spending a bit more on toner."

M. Sanwell, St Albans

Photocopier Stepladder – It's what photocopiers were meant for.

Planning a long run? Try our Photocopier Back Support

 Can I work from home?

Can I work from home?

Can I work from home?

Everybody Can Work From Home with

Office Wendy Pro

Now With Chimney!

Bargain Hunt; Cash In The Attic; The Jeremy Kyle Show— no wonder everybody wants to work from home these days. But are constant requests from your staff to be allowed to work from home driving you mad? Problem solved, with Office Wendy Pro.

Office Wendy Pro is a desktop home from home for office professionals who want to experience the thrill of working from home, but who can't be trusted to get on unsupervised.

Featuring four windows, a door and - for the first time - a chimney, the surprisingly spacious single-level accommodation comes with all the furnishings and conveniences of a real home painted onto the interior walls.

As an office professional, being told you're not allowed to work from home can leave you feeling like a naughty boy - this is much more grown up.

We've been trusted to work from home

Get help making up new acronyms with

Acronym Boggle

As any manager will testify, waiting for head office to create new and exciting acronyms for the workplace can feel like an eternity. Well, now you can create your own in seconds thanks to Acronym Boggle.

Acronym Boggle has been specially created to help managers like you create their very own exciting and fresh-sounding acronyms. Simply shake the letters, say what you see, and start creating your very own nationally and internationally recognised acronyms.

Shake 'n' Make!

SWAD FIG GYMP TYRD

GIFFY TWANG TRMPTN

... and many, many more!

Good morning, everyone. Just to remind you that the purpose of today's meeting is to come up with some new acronyms to ensure mission clarity moving forward into the future. Sue has already shaken the letters so, shall we begin?

SKYD!

SMRG!

SCRTM!

New for Office Managers ...

Collapsing Employee

Coping

Thumb-Activated Collapsing Employees for Office Managers

Not coping very well

Not coping at all well

It's one of the most rewarding aspects of being a manager - giving an employee too much work to do and then watching them collapse. Well, now you can enjoy it time and time again thanks to Collapsing Employee.

Collapsing Employees are beautifully crafted, hand-made wooden toys for mid- to high-level managers. Simply press the base to see the employee collapse. Parts are connected with string; when base is pressed up the employee will collapse. Move base up and down rapidly to see the employee dance and jiggle.

Ha ha ha ha ha! Look at him collapse!

Management Reviews:

"I love keeping them at the 'not coping very well' stage - hilarious." C. Parker, Taunton

"Very, very funny - can't get it off my 3-year old." P. Jenkins, Ipswich

Ha ha! Falling down's funny with Collapsing Employee!

It's 'Goodbye' and 'Good Riddance' with an

Honesty Card

Saying goodbye to a long-standing and much-loved colleague can be an emotional time. But what if the back of a colleague is something you've wanted to see for years? Time to give an Honesty Card.

Honesty Cards are the perfect way to say 'goodbye' to colleagues you never really got on with. Each Honesty Card comes with a refreshingly honest farewell message enabling you to say a frank goodbye to work-mates you never really liked. Choose from 6 refreshingly frank designs:

Good Luck!

message inside reads:

...not really. I hope things turn out really badly for you.

You're moving onto pastures new...

message inside reads:

...bit like a cow.

It's time for you to take another path...

message inside reads:

...may I suggest a crumbling cliff-top one?

It's time to say Goodbye...

Message inside reads:

...wish I could have said it years ago.

Be Honest for just £2.50 each

I hear you're leaving us

message inside reads:

Good.

So You're Leaving...

message inside reads:

...it's probably for the best – only the other day a large group of us were talking about you and nobody said anything nice.

An End To Unwanted Intimacy with

Inflatable Chest

As a person with a full set of social skills you wouldn't dream of entering somebody else's personal space. Sadly, there are people who work in offices who don't regard the 20 or so inches directly in front of another person as already psychologically taken. So what do you do when somebody in the workplace routinely violates your intimate zone? – get an Inflatable Chest!

Inflatable Chest provides an impenetrable first line of defence against personal-space invaders. One tug on the ripcord causes the chest to gradually swell, gently encouraging socially inept colleagues to leave your personal space and not come back. Take back what's rightfully yours with Inflatable Chest.

Office Review: Absolutely brilliant – comes in handy with the wife, too. S. Donald, Rye

Morning John, mind if I stand on your feet and breathe on you?

I'd rather you didn't, if it's all the same with you.

TUG!

Only £127

Freedom is just one tug away with Inflatable Chest!

Is Cheap Office Furniture Holding You Back? Time for
A Touch of Wood

It's a common complaint: office professionals not being taken seriously in the workplace due to the cheap construction of their office furniture - thank goodness for A Touch of Wood.

A Touch of Wood is a range of sticky-back solid wood-effect coverings specially designed to add a veneer of respectability to even the most cheaply constructed office furniture. Simply cut to size, apply to your cheaply constructed office furniture and start getting taken seriously.

Get Wood Today!
Choose from 3 luxury wood effects:

Fauxoak

Get Wood Today!

Walnot

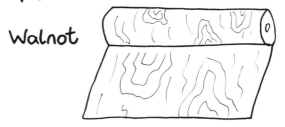

Nohogany

It's great for making colleagues needlessly jealous, too!

Why should I?

Because I said so. And because I have an oak desk.

John, he's got a point.

Wow! Mahogany bin - have you been promoted?

I'm not supposed to say anything but I think it's pretty clear the company is investing in me.

Boardroom-level office furnishing from just £14.99 per roll!

Put An End To Toilet Jollies with a

Toilet Spider

Mind if I join you, Sharon?

According to research from The Institute of Economic Studies, employees going to the toilet when they don't really need to costs the economy over £7 billion a year. So if your staff are spending too much time on the wrong job perhaps it's time you got a Toilet Spider.

Toilet Spiders are specially bred for their thick leg hair and large, scary bodies, and are just perfect for turning a toilet jolly into an ordeal not to be prolonged.

Stop losing money to toilet jollies today!

AAAARRGGHH!

Knickers, Mrs Lamb

Not So Jolly Now!

I'll put a stop to unnecessary and lavishly proportioned toilet breaks

Also from the people that brought you Toilet Spider: U-Bend Crabs Would You Risk It?

Transparent Stationery- Cupboard Door

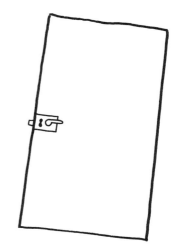

There's nothing more corrosive to harmony in the workplace than gossip and rumour. What starts as a bit of neighbourly curiosity into other people's private lives quickly leads to speculation and making things up. The problem: nobody really knows who's getting off with who; the solution: a Transparent Stationery-Cupboard Door.

A Transparent Stationery-Cupboard Door is the perfect way to keep staff from having to make things up about other people's private lives whilst allowing everyone to share the thrill and excitement of an office romance that has nothing to do with them. A large, clear, perspex door affords excellent viewing from outside whilst a lock ensures a sense of privacy and dignity for courting couples.

Aw! Isn't it nice to see?

Yes, it is - do you think I've put enough chairs out?

Everyone Can Enjoy an Office Romance with a Transparent Stationery- Cupboard Door - Just £67

Somebody Else's Family Portrait

It's a popular feature in any office – the family portrait placed on the desk as a reminder that the slog is worth it. But does looking at a picture of your own wife and kids leave you wondering if it actually is? If so, you need Somebody Else's Family Portrait.

At Somebody Else's Family Portrait we'll give you a family you'll be only too happy to work like a slave for. Simply send us a passport-sized photo of yourself and we'll scan your face onto one of our thousands of model family portraits.

Get the family you've always dreamed of...

Beautiful wife...

Normal-looking kids...

obedient dog...

... the only thing missing is you!

Your wife – she's a very beautiful lady.

It's not my wife, my wife's ugly.

**Somebody Else's Family Portrait –
A Family Worth the Effort**

Hey, great-looking kid – makes it all worthwhile doesn't it?

D'you know, that little fella's the only thing that keeps me going sometimes – my own son's a waste of space.

Clear the air in your office

Washing Hint
Flannel &   Soap Gift Set

No one likes to tell a colleague they smell of B.O. so give them a helping hint with the Washing Hint Flannel and Soap Gift Set.

The Washing Hint Flannel and Soap Gift Set contains everything necessary for the prevention of unsavoury smells - that's a flannel and some soap - each bearing the eye-catching Washing Hint logo. And because it comes in a beautiful presentation gift box it's perfect for Christmas and birthdays.

Washing Hint
Flannel & Soap
Gift Set

Washing Hint

Washing Hint

Say It With Soap!

It's Just A Suggestion

This beautifully presented gift box really took the edge off being told I smelled.

Office Review: "Admittedly I wasn't washing but I had no idea I'd actually started to smell. Thank goodness for Secret Santa!"

C. Bridger, Notts

"Of course I'd noticed the smell too, but I hadn't linked it to my not washing. Fortunately, my colleagues had - thanks guys."

P. Flanders, Cumbria

The Washing Hint Flannel & Soap Gift Set - because some people need help remembering to wash.

Oooo! Smelly

Yes, a bit

...but this should help

Start a germ co-operative at your place of work

Agar Germ Exchange

Lick for days off!

Is your immune system annoyingly robust?
Do you have difficulty becoming ill?
Do viruses give you a wide berth?

If the answer to one or more of these questions is 'yes' then perhaps it's time to get an Agar Germ Exchange.

An Agar Germ Exchange is the friendly way for colleagues to share bugs and germs with one another, helping everyone in the office to achieve a much-coveted day-off-sick.

Easy to use: Simply ask colleagues to lick the bacteria-producing jelly at the first sign of illness and let the Agar Germ Exchange produce a sickness bug that you can all enjoy.

Start a germ co-operative in your office and help colleagues enjoy the many benefits of a day in front of the telly.

Office Reviews:

"People forget – there's a lot more choice nowadays; a day at home doesn't have to mean Murder She Wrote or Pebble Mill at One anymore. Definitely worth a lick."
S. Sayer, Rochdale

"Was 24 hours' diarrhoea and vomiting worth two Bargain Hunts and an all-new Trisha with all 3 kids at school? I'd say so."
P. Kelly, Wakefield

I've just posted a lovely bit of Norovirus, Cathy.

Ooh, lovely. Jeremy Kyle tomorrow.

Give the team a lift with
Team-Lift Doughnuts

Create a Sugar Rush of Enthusiasm!

Is your team a bit sad and droopy?

Give them a lift with Team-Lift Doughnuts!

Team-Lift Doughnuts are motivational doughnuts specially designed to raise the morale of sad and droopy teams. Each one bears an iced message specially worded to lift jaded teams, whilst the jam filling provides each and every team member with a reason to go on.

Team-Lift Doughnuts

Contains 5 Team-Lift Doughnuts

Mission Impossible — You Can Do It!

Think Doughnut and Go For It!

Jam – a reason to hit all your sales targets

The secret of getting ahead is getting started – enjoy your doughnut

Winners never quit — mind you don't get jam on your trousers

Jam, at last, a reason to go on

Are you harnessing the amazing power of doughnuts?

Doughnuts!

Let's dance

You could lift a team of five out of misery for less than £1

You'd be amazed what a doughnut can do!

There's More To Work Than Working with

Piano Fingers

Knitting, gaming, sending flirty texts - they're all things you could be doing under your desk instead of getting on with your work. And now you can be thanks to Piano Fingers.

Piano Fingers are pneumatically operated typing hands for employees who want to get on with things other than their work.

* Not to scale. For illustrative purposes only.

Simply place Piano Fingers over your keyboard, pin the decoy sleeves to the top of each shoulder and start doing things you enjoy under your desk. When management approaches simply operate the treadle and make Piano Fingers make you look busy.

Just think, what could you be doing under your desk instead of getting on with your work?

Piano Fingers - because there's more to work than working.

Say 'Thanks but no thanks' with a

Consolation Cupcake

It's always been a managerial hot cake–fending off staff's ridiculous suggestions without wanting to hurt their feelings. If only there was a gentler way of telling people their ideas are rubbish. Well, now there is with Consolation Cupcakes.

Consolation Cupcakes are the perfect way to thank team members for their useless suggestions without damaging team cohesion and staff morale. Each cupcake bears an iced message of condolence helping people to feel better about the worthlessness of their input at what can be a difficult period of rejection.

12 ever-so thoughtful ways to say 'No thanks'

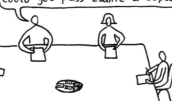

Office Review:

"Work a treat at home, too, though the wife is getting a little fat, now." A. Lynch, Inverness

Consolation Cupcakes– Consolatory Confection for Rubbish Ideas

Is it time you got a Tea Bitch?

Are you one of the millions of office professionals not being taken seriously in the workplace because you still have to make your own cup of tea? Perhaps it's time you got a tea bitch.

Perhaps It's Time You Got A Tea Bitch is the outstanding new book by leading self-actualization guru Pashma Namru. In it he convincingly argues that being able to direct someone to make you a cup of tea without them telling you to sod off suggests management potential and can give you the confidence needed to secure that promotion.

Packed full of practical advice and helpful ideas, this book will show you just how easy it is to manipulate workmates into being your very own tea bitch.

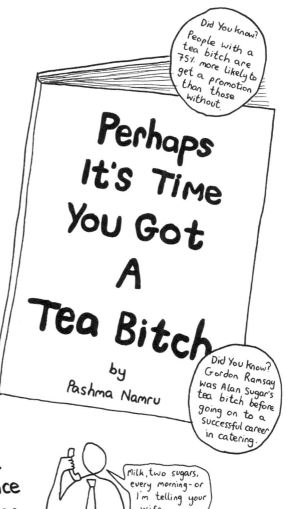

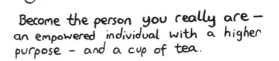

Become the person you really are — an empowered individual with a higher purpose - and a cup of tea.

Are You Somebody Else's Tea Bitch? Fight back with

Sticky Coasters

sticky Coating

Peel 'n' Place

About time, too, I've been gagging for one of these all morning

Being somebody else's tea bitch is one of the toughest jobs out there: standing, stirring, carrying - it can be hell, not to mention humiliating. So if you're suffering under the heavy yoke of a cruel tea master perhaps it's time you started insisting on coasters- Sticky Coasters!

Sticky Coasters are specially designed to stay stuck to the mug when lifted, revealing a childish text or image visible to all but the drinker. So, if you want to fight back against your tea master, isn't it time you started to insist on

Sticky Coasters?

Is the coaster really necessary?

I believe it is, Mr Sugar

Choose from...

I'm a 🔔 end

I'm drinking hen's wee- how about you?

Your chin reminds me of cottage cheese

Start insisting on coasters-Sticky Coasters!

Is one of your colleagues bringing their Job to work with them?

Find out who it is with

Muck Chimes
keep the morning clean

Picture the scene: the inbox is empty, the presentation is ready, the report is on the boss's table and the coffee is on. Sunshine is streaming through the window and a glance at the clock tells you that it's still only eight thirty. What could possibly spoil such a morning as this? Answer: the smell of excrement wafting through the building.

As a reasonable person you wouldn't dream of deliberately taking your turd to work with you. Unfortunately, some people would — the result: stench, and the morning ruined.

Fortunately there is a solution — Muck Chimes! Muck Chimes are a stool alarm system specifically designed to catch colleagues who bring their Jobs to work with them.

Muck Chimes are slightly weighted so they won't tinkle if you only sprinkle. But attempt any weightier business and you'll be - quite literally - creating a cacophony. Simply suspend Muck Chimes across the bowl of your work's toilet and secure in place with the chains and padlock provided.

What, so I'm supposed to stand here all day listening for chimes?

That's right - or find somewhere else to do your work experience.

Did you know? Muck-chiming was first practised by the ancient Chinese to ensure purity in temples and sacred places.

Find out who's ruining your pre-work quiet-time with

Muck Chimes – keep the morning clean

Warning: May Cause Soiling

Line-of-Sight Pillars

It's something that people with desks behind pillars have known for a long time – if your boss can't see you, you don't have to do as much work. Now, thanks to Line-of-Sight Pillars, you too can enjoy the many benefits of not having to do as much work as other people.

Available in 5 attractive shades of grey, Line-of-Sight Pillars offer a generous 36-inch screening capability giving you all the protection you need to book flights, send flirty texts or simply rest.

What's more, Line-of-Sight Pillars' lightweight polystyrene construction means that taking a piece of weight-bearing architecture into work to hide behind has never been easier.

Only £100 each

I've got the new temp in reception, shall I send him across?

Line-of-Sight Pillars – because you not doing any work is the last thing you want your boss to see.

A new denim look for every staff social with

Dressing In Denim

– for men who manage

As a senior-level manager you hardly need reminding to wear jeans to all staff socials – they're cool, they're trendy and they help you to fit in with people you've got nothing in common with. But are you getting the most out of your denim?

Dressing In Denim is a brand new, bi-monthly magazine for men who manage, but who also want to get the most out of the denim in their wardrobe. Packed full of handy tips and ideas, Dressing In Denim will help you breathe new life into your cheap, outdated and badly cut denim, giving you

Dressing In Denim

– for men who manage

Inside this issue:

P16 Triple Denim – make it work for you!

P27 – Times not to wear stonewashed (There isn't one, stupid!)

P42 – Jeans with work shoes

P63 – Frosted Wash We meet the MDs still keeping it cool

P74 – Going Naked Losing that belt at weddings

P96 – Massive Buckles – How to get your crotch noticed: we review 10 of the biggest (buckles, not crotches)

Free Western bolo tie with this issue

Exclusive Interview: Status Quo frontman Francis Rossi on jeans with high-top trainers

a fresh, new, dressed-down look for every staff social occasion. Birthday drinks? Office Party? Wedding disco? Dress to look great and fit in with Dressing In Denim.

A fresh, new, slightly awkward middle-age jean look in every issue

Subscribe today and get 25% off **Office Dance Party II** – festive dance moves for people who manage.

Dressing In Denim – why look like you don't fit in when you can dress in denim?

Motivational Posters

If you're not motivating your staff then you're not getting the most out of them, so give your team a motivational boost with this stunning set of inspirational posters.

Each poster displays a recognised motivational image – mountaintop, skydiver, climber dangling from an overhang – along with a simple and easy to remember motivational message. Simply mount them on the walls of your office space and start reaping the benefits of a highly motivated workforce.

Opportunity... ...comes to those who are prepared to stay late

Put In More Effort

Be Strong

Put The Company First

Overcome Obstacles... ...before they overcome you and you lose your job

Look! A Sky-Diver

Makes you want to work weekends, doesn't it?

Work Harder

Try To Do More

Have you tried our Motivational Urinal Blocks?

Believe in Yourself! only you can make it happen Aim Higher

What could urinal motivation mean for your annual turnover?

Motivation – It's what management's all about

Get Organised In The Office with a

Round Filing Cabinet

Drowning in paperwork?

Flooded by forms?

Sinking in sheets?

Then perhaps it's time that your office was fitted with a Round Filing Cabinet.

Round Filing Cabinet is the instant solution for work that you simply haven't got time to do. Just put all the work that you can't do into Round Filing Cabinet, leave it overnight outside a door or in another prominent place and when you come back in the morning you'll no longer have that work to do - guaranteed!

Work goes here

Round Filing Cabinet

Going... Going... Gone! - Makes Even Hard Work Disappear!

Office Reviews:

"I simply put all of the work I couldn't do into Round Filing Cabinet and by the next morning it was gone - done, one presumes."

R. Nicholas, Yately

"I've been using Round Filing Cabinets for over six months now. One evening I decided to stay late to see how my work was being done. I waited until the cleaners arrived and then gave up. I still have no idea who's doing my work."

G. Fraser, Exeter

Round Filing Cabinet

It Does The Work You Can't

Get Organised - Get Filing!

A Plague On Time Thieves with

Anti-Time-Thief Scabs & Sores

A teenage daughter gap-year anecdote; some detailed DIY advice you didn't ask for and have no need of; an unusually boring story, involving nobody you know... Sound familiar? If so you've probably been hit by a time thief.

Time thieves operate wherever there are busy people trying to get on with things. They prey on good-natured, patient people, waylaying their victims with trivial and unnecessary conversation whilst helping themselves to hour after hour of their time. They have only one weakness — like many of us, time thieves don't like talking to people with scabs and sores around their mouths.

Introducing... Anti-Time-Thief Scabs and Sores!

Anti-Time-Thief Scabs and Sores provide unrivalled protection against

office time thieves. Simply select a dozen or so scabs and sores, peel off the backings and apply to the mouth area paying particular attention to the mouth corners. And that's it, you're now ready to stand up to your office time thief:

Scabs & Sores — an end to daylight robbery!

An End To Office Snog Ruts with the

Don't leave Love to chance

Christmas Party Love Planner

Alcohol, overtly sexual dancing, a finger-buffet — we all know where it can lead: there's nothing like the office Christmas Party for getting off with a colleague. But are you finding that you're getting off with the same colleague year after year? Then plan for change with the Christmas Party Love Planner!

Couple No.	Partners		Finger Buffet	Grope opt-In
1	A	Val	✓	
	B	Brian	✓	
2	A	Sue	✗	✓
	B	Richard	✓	✓
3	A	Kay	✓	
	B	Mike	✗	✓

The Christmas Party Love Planner - 2014

The Christmas Party Love Planner has been specially designed to ensure that office romantics like you don't get stuck in a year-on-year snog rut.

Would-be lovers register an interest with their line manager and their names are entered into a draw. The results of the draw are then entered onto the Love Planner showing office party snoggers exactly who the free bar is going to make them fall in love with

this year. There's even a grope opt-in facility!

No.14

No.14 - Sharon from HR - will snog...

No. 7

No.7 - Peter from Finance

Give everyone a crack at a cracker this Christmas with the Christmas Party Love Planner

Be honest to yourself about lying to others with

Honesty Nose

Telling lies to staff - it's the not-so-secret magic ingredient for maintaining a happy and well-motivated work-force. But what if telling lies to your staff all day is beginning to make you feel dishonest? Honesty Nose could help.

Honesty Nose is a Pinocchio-inspired, fib-shaped nose for managers who want to enjoy the many benefits of not telling their staff the truth, without wanting to feel like a person who tells lies.

Pulled over the nose for lie-telling, Honesty Nose enables managers and team leaders like you to be honest to yourself at a time when you're not being honest to others. Honesty Nose - tell your staff the lies they love to hear without being false to yourself.

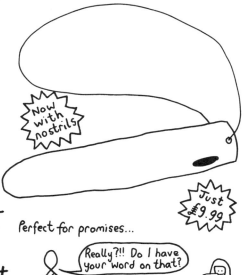

Now with nostrils

Just £9.99

Perfect for promises...

Really?!! Do I have your word on that?

You have my word.

Great for morale...

Does my bum look big in this skirt?

Hold on a minute.

Office Review: "Starting to believe your own lies is one of the many hazards of management; fortunately Honesty Nose helped me see right from wrong."
P. Siddle, Staffs.

Ideal for meetings...

I'm delighted to announce there will be no compulsory redundancies.

Hooray! Our jobs are safe!

Honesty Nose

It's honest-to-goodness no-nonsense not telling the truth!

Fail to meet deadlines sooner with

Completion Date Forwarder

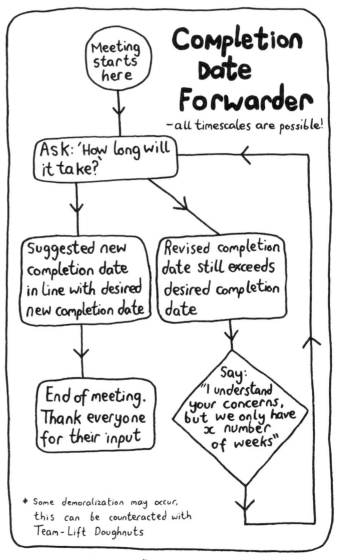

All timescales are possible!

As a project manager you've never been in the business of meeting the unrealistic deadlines you set. But now you could be failing to meet those deadlines even sooner thanks to Completion Date Forwarder.

Completion Date Forwarder features a reasoning loop specially developed to encourage 'full-team buy-in' to poorly thought-through last-minute deadline changes. Simply announce a meeting, inform your team that the project completion date needs to be brought forward and then follow the directions on the flow diagram until your team 'embrace reality'. And remember, pretending to write down your team's concerns helps achieve that all-important 'full-team buy-in'.

Completion Date Forwarder
– all timescales are possible!

Meeting starts here

Ask: 'How long will it take?'

Suggested new completion date in line with desired new completion date

Revised completion date still exceeds desired completion date

End of meeting. Thank everyone for their input

Say: "I understand your concerns, but we only have x number of weeks"

*Some demoralization may occur, this can be counteracted with Team-Lift Doughnuts

Office Review: "I managed to get a six-month project down to two weeks in under five minutes - Embrace Reality!"
S. Andrews, Redcar

Report not done? Sales figures down? Baby not sleeping? What you need is a nice cup of

Somebody Else's Coffee

Admit it, after a tough morning in the office there's nothing quite like the taste of somebody else's coffee. That's why Somebody Else's Coffee has been specially roasted to give you that unique taste of coffee that doesn't belong to you.

Sit back, relax, and enjoy the unmistakeable flavour of coffee that doesn't belong to you with Somebody Else's Coffee.

If you enjoy the taste of Somebody Else's Coffee then why not try other products from Tea Break Solutions:

Somebody Else's Tea
Somebody Else's Milk
& Somebody Else's Biscuits

Somebody Else's Coffee

It Just tastes better

Somebody Else's Mug Offer

Collect 6 Tokens and you could be drinking Somebody Else's Coffee from Somebody Else's Mug — there's nothing quite like the taste of Somebody Else's Coffee from Somebody Else's Mug.

Just 6 Tokens plus £5.99 postage & packing.

End Every Day on a High with

Valium Salt-Lick

- Does a day in the office make you tense and irritable?
- Are you frequently found crying in the toilet?
- Do you want to hit people you work with?

If the answer to any of these questions is yes then perhaps it's time you asked your boss for a Valium Salt-Lick.

For thousands of years farmers have been using salt-licks to keep cattle and horses happy and healthy. Now you too can enjoy the many health benefits of a salty deposit with all the added goodness of Valium.

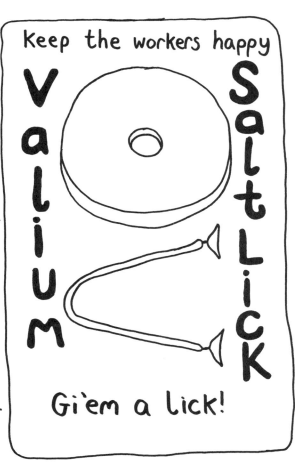

keep the workers happy

Valium Salt Lick

Gi'em a lick!

Don't let the cleaners have it all.

Valium Salt-Lick – It's Management Made Easy!

Also from the makers of Valium Salt-Lick...

Valipops

Adult treats for office professionals

Gi's a lick!

Face every day the Valipop way!

Tea-cooling tips for managers with

Jobs To Make Their Tea Go Cold

When a junior colleague sits down in front of you with a steaming mug of tea, thoughts naturally turn to finding them a job to do until it goes cold. But what if coming up with spurious tea-cooling tasks is not one of your managerial strengths? Jobs To Make Their Tea Go Cold could help.

Jobs To Make Their Tea Go Cold is packed full of useful ideas guaranteed to occupy junior colleagues while their tea goes cold. From a first-floor staple count, to measuring the perimeter of the office with a piece of string, Jobs To Make Their Tea Go Cold is the seminal text for office managers who don't like having hot cups of tea drunk in front of them.

Jobs To Make Their Tea Go Cold

Did you know it takes an average of 23 minutes for a hot cup of tea to lose all of its enjoyable qualities?

Jake, sorry to land this on you, I've just had Head Office on the phone; I need you to do 23 minutes' worth of stock-take -bit of an emergency. Leave your tea there -have it when you get back.

It's not cold tea that bothers us -we haven't got a problem with that. It's hot, enjoyable tea that bothers us.

Jobs To Make Their Tea Go Cold

Helping you to help tea go cold

Discover Your Lost Personality with the

Cartoon Tie and Sock Co.

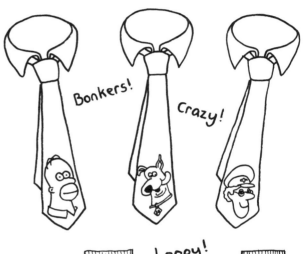

As an office employee you'll be the first to admit that you're a bit boring: emails, reports, squabbling over staplers – it's not easy to develop and maintain even a basic personality. Answer: Cartoon Ties and Socks!

At The Cartoon Tie and Sock Company we've been supplying office professionals with hilarious, quirky and fun-loving personalities since 1982. From Hong Kong Phooey to The Simpsons, from Postman Pat to Scooby-Doo, our exhaustive range of cartoon ties and socks is guaranteed to contain the zany, crazy, fun-loving personality you've always craved. Don't delay – order your surrogate personality today!

Bonkers!

Crazy!

Loopy!

Mental!

I'm hilarious to be around, are you?

You and your cartoon ties, you're bonkers you are - a real card. Not like all the rest, they haven't got a sense of humour at all, not like you. They're all so boring and serious, but you're not, you're really funny. And quirky.

Cartoon Socks and Ties - for the complete office personality

Pass it on with...
Cascader

Have you ever noticed, work is better when somebody else is doing it? Well, now they could be thanks to Cascader.

Cascader is the perfect way to share unwanted and hard-to-do work with colleagues working beneath you. A precision funnel delivers work directly onto a powerful allocation fan whilst an impressive 4.6 metre capability makes for spectacular and wide load distribution. We've even fitted a splash guard to reduce nuisance comeback.

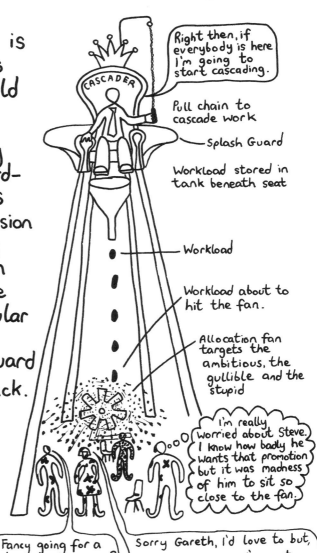

What's more, Cascader's unique under-seat storage facility allows you to collect and save the very best cascadable material before delivering it all in one impressive and memorable sitting.

Start Cascading Today!

Office Review: "I can hardly express the pleasure I get from cascading on my staff." R. Huntly, Worksop

Cascader — purchase yours today for just £2999

Self-Wedgie Prevention with
Anti-Wedgie Stirrups

If you're one of the hundreds of thousands of office professionals who struggle each day not to pull the crotch of their trousers into a socially compromising place, then Anti-Wedgie Stirrups are just the thing for you.

Anti-Wedgie Stirrups are powerful elasticated straps specially designed to prevent self-wedgiers from pulling up their trousers to unacceptable levels. Simply clip each stirrup onto a trouser leg, locate the straps under the instep of each foot and immediately start enjoying all the benefits of not appearing to have wedged your trousers into your arse crack.

Office Review:"People think the stirrups will be uncomfortable - let me tell you, they're a lot less uncomfortable than having your trousers wedged up your arse all day." F. Bradley, Isle of Man

Gentlemen, you have identical qualifications and your reputations are equally without blemish - John, I'd like to give you the job.

Thank you

...and thank you, too, Anti-Wedgie stirrups

Also from Wedgie Products...
The 'Too-High' Tie

The dressing-time reminder for people who self-wedgie

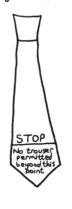

STOP No trouser permitted beyond this point

Whip it away with...

Flay-Away

Whip Yourself Clean!

Do you sometimes get home before 9.00 p.m?

Did you take your full allocation of annual leave last year?

Have you ever left the office early just to see a rubbishy school play?

We've all done something unprofessional before, but the feeling of guilt isn't nice, is it? Well, now you can whip that guilt away with Flay-Away.

Flay-Away is a self-mortification device for office professionals suffering from feelings of guilt associated with not putting the company first. Anytime, anywhere, Flay-Away enables you to simply and easily administer the punishment you deserve, providing instant relief from feelings of guilt and helping you to accept corporate forgiveness.

whip your corporate sins away for just £31

Ruddy Sports Days

Start Receiving Corporate Forgiveness Today!

Got a commitment you simply can't get out of but worried about the guilt? Try one of our Hair Shirts

Great for funerals!

model shown: The Thomas à Becket £22

Done a fart? Need Someone to Blame? You Need

Instant Work-Experience Kid

Come on, we've all done it - let rip at work thinking there's no one around only to freeze in horror at the words, 'Ah, there you are!' Well, now there's someone to take the blame for your reckless stench-making — Instant Work-Experience kid!

Just one tug on Instant Work-Experience kid's secret string causes him to rapidly inflate, instantly providing you with someone who's only too happy for you to have one on him.

'Have one on me!'

Also from the makers of Instant Work-Experience kid...

... Instant Dog

and

Instant Baby

'Have one on us!'

Ah, there you are, Pauline.

oh no! I bet the room reeks of guff - better activate Instant Work-Experience kid.

Is that you, Connor, you disgusting ape? I really must apologise, Mr Henderson.

Be stench Blameless for Just £39.99

Glazed-in Grievances for Office Grumblers with

Dirty Cups

A person with a grievance is always happy, so give your office grumbler something to moan about with Dirty Cups.

Dirty Cups come with glazed-in tea, coffee and lipstick stains giving them the not-washed-up-properly look that office grumblers love to complain about.

This month only – 10 heavy-duty laminator pouches with every order - Absolutely Free!

Review: "Such was the intensity of feeling regarding the dirty cups that I was able to implement a 10% pay cut without a murmur of opposition." G. Fraser, Thurso

Also from Dirty Cups...

...Dirty Plates – think, what could a glazed-in ketchup or yolk stain do for your company? Now with PermaCrumb

Happiness is just a glazed-in stain away

Give Yourself the Pay Rise You Deserve with a
Fake Pay Slip

How would you feel if you found out that a colleague was being paid more than you for doing the same job? Exactly! – so what are you waiting for? Get yourself on the right end of some petty office jealousy with a Fake Pay Slip.

At The Fake Pay Slip Company we have over 15 years' experience of doctoring employee pay slips to create petty and needless office jealousy.

Simply send us one of your old pay slips, tell us what you'd like others to think you're earning, and we'll send you an amended pay slip to leave lying around the office.

Become the principal object of jealous loathing in your office – today!

Give Independent Thinking the Stimulation it Deserves

with Thought Probe

Annoying, isn't it? – Junior members of staff coming up with good ideas. Not only does it ride roughshod over long-established office hierarchies, it can also leave senior members of staff like you looking like they don't know what they're doing. But what should you do if the good ideas in your company keep coming from people not paid enough to be clever? Answer: Get a Thought Probe.

a powerful 2000 volt shock, causing maverick thinkers to temporarily lose their train of thought whilst saving the honour of senior members of staff like you.

Thought Probe is an electric-shock thought-prevention device designed to eradicate the independent thinking that can lead to un- wanted good ideas. When applied to the head the probe delivers

Finally! – An end to other people's good ideas with **Thought Probe**

Help Plan Unforeseen Staff Absences

with a Staff Sickness Rota

A member of staff off sick at short notice can cause havoc in the office, but did you know that 90% of staff know when they're going to be ill? That's right, 90%! So why not start planning staff sickness in your office with the help of a staff Sickness Rota?

The Staff Sickness Rota allows staff to roster-in days-off-due-to-illness up to 6 months in advance, helping office managers plan for unforeseen absences and take a tough stance on sick leave.

Staff Sickness Rota

Name	Illness	Date(s)	Will you require a get well soon card?
Brian	Tummy upset	21st-22nd April	No
Cathy	Sore throat (quite a bad one)	6th August	Yes, I think so
Anne	My youngest is going to be off school with earache	15th May	I think she'd really appreciate that, thanks
Sam	TBC	Sometime in the first week of June	No
Kate	Headache, vomiting, tiredness... general midweek hangover	5th August	No ta!

John, according to the rota you've got a bad cold today; I really don't think you're well enough to be here.

How stupid of me, no wonder I'm not feeling very well.

Get Tough on sickness!

I'm down to have a cold next Tuesday, Trish, but I don't think I'm going to get it now; I think I'm going to get it the week after if that's ok?

I'm sorry, Sue, Peter in accounting's already having an earache that week and I can't afford to lose you both to staff sickness

Expect the Unexpected with a Staff Sickness Rota Just

Get help starting malicious gossip with

Rumour Cards

For lovers of office gossip and rumour, colleagues not having affairs at work can be a real problem. But now, thanks to Rumour Cards, practisers of marital faithfulness need never again leave office gossipmongers with nothing to talk about.

Rumour Cards help malicious gossips working in unfavourable conditions to come up with the sensational rumours we all love to hear, despite the monogamy of others.

Each pack of Rumour Cards contains a wealth of possible names, locations and props, specially chosen to appeal to people who like to make things up. To find out who's been doing what with whom in your office, simply shuffle the pack and make a reading:

Want more gossip? Simply play more cards –

Mrs Peacock, with Brian from Accounts, in the meeting room, with the rope and the candlestick – sensational!

I knew it.

So did I. Who's Brian?

John, from Finance, with Mrs White, by the photocopier.

Sharon! You'll never guess what.

If you can't deal with the truth, start dealing in rumour with Rumour Cards

Competition

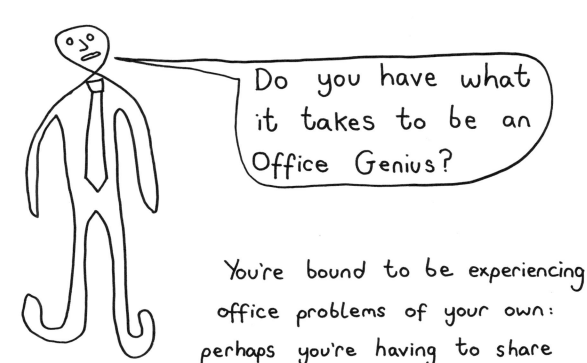

Do you have what it takes to be an Office Genius?

You're bound to be experiencing office problems of your own: perhaps you're having to share an office with someone who's better looking than you are, or maybe you're having to work alongside a colleague who's got an ever so slightly bigger desk than you, even though you've been with the company longer than them.

Whatever the particular evil you're suffering under, send your genius solution to @Summersdale with the hashtag #OfficeGenius and the person who comes up with our favourite will win something nice.

ISBN: 978 1 84953 359 1 • Paperback • £9.99

Marking, planning, stealing colleagues' milk – teaching has always been a difficult job. Now, with this outrageous catalogue of teaching aids, the **times educational miscreant** shares his unique approach to many of teaching's most taxing problems.

Whether it's marking coursework by weight with Coursework Scales, or planning lessons with the Page-Choosing Money Box, *The Art of Teaching* is an absolute must for the conscientious teaching professional.

If you're interested in finding out more about our books,
find us on Facebook at **Summersdale Publishers**
and follow us on Twitter at **@Summersdale**.

www.summersdale.com